How to build a

HOUSE OF HEARTS

♥ **Doris Jasinek and Pamela Bell Ryan** ♥

Illustrated by Caroline Price

CompCare®
Publishers

Jasinek, Doris.
    How to build a house of hearts: a heart-level home makes everyone
who lives there feel good/Doris Jasinek, Pamela Bell Ryan.

        p.   cm.
    ISBN 0-89638-147-1 : $5.95
    1. Parenting—United States.   2. Parent and child—United States.
I. Ryan, Pamela Bell.   II. Title.
HQ755.8.J37 1988
    646.7'8—dc19   88-11839
                        CIP

Illustrations by Caroline Price
Cover and interior design by MacLean & Tuminelly

Inquiries, orders, and catalog requests should be addressed to
CompCare Publishers
2415 Annapolis Lane
Minneapolis, Minnesota 55441
Call toll free 800/328-3330
Minnesota residents 612/559-4800

    6   5   4   3   2   1
    93   92   91   90   89   88

A Heartbook, Not a Handbook

Creating a warm family climate in which children and adults alike can feel loved and needed and grow as individuals—that's one of life's biggest challenges. Theories abound. Psychologists invent new terms. And in the tangle of all these "solutions," sometimes the real answers get lost.

This unique little book reminds us gently—and simply—that the best and most practical guidelines for everyday family living come straight from the heart.

Build a heart-level home.

To our mothers,
Hilda Brethorst and Hope Bell,
who let us be.
And to our children,
who are being in spite of us.

Hugs to Gary and Jim
for their cooperation
and love.

Start to build a house of hearts.

From Heart to Heart

Living in a family — trying to do what's best for children and adults too — has its dilemmas and uncertainties.

Being a parent is particularly perplexing. And depending on the experts doesn't always make it easier. Parents are tempted to listen mostly to *their* parents — or their peers. Or to practice textbook psychologies.

> "Mom, can't I stay up? I know eight o'clock's my bedtime,
> but Daddy's coming home from the airport. Pleeease, Mom.
> I won't be tired in the morning!"

Grandma says kids should be in bed by eight. The neighbors' kids never stay up late. The books say be consistent. Sometimes intellectual approaches tell you what you should do and contradict what you feel.

Listen to your heart.

Play: A Gift from the Heart

"Hey, look what I made! A castle 'way up to the sky. I put lots and lots of leaves up on top—they can be flags. Hey, you want to play too? We can make a birthday cake—a great big birthday cake 'way up to the sky, with candles on top. There. I know...let's smash it down. You're my friend, okay? Hey, look what we made!"

Old-fashioned play is rare in our high-tech, cerebral world. Remember card-table forts? Backyard theaters? Lemonade stands?

Play helps a child find out who he is or where she fits in. In fact, play is a child's most important activity. Through play, children encounter their world and deal with it at their level. Through play, they learn logical thinking and problem-solving. They develop their senses and their muscles. They learn how to get along with each other. For a child, play is a more profound experience than most adults realize.

Many parents feel pressured to launch a three-year-old in the direction of a Ph.D. By focusing on what they think is best for the child's future, they miss what is best for right now. Childhood is the time for play.

And play is a time for experiencing the joys of water, sand, paint, and paper. It is a time for dirt under fingernails that come clean only after playing in the tub until the skin is wrinkly. Dirt and water are a kid's best friends.

Don't get hung up on being grown-up.

Play isn't reserved *just* for children. You don't have to act the role of adult all the time. Reach for the child within. When a silly or whimsical situation arises, enjoy it — giggle, dance, sing, wrestle, pretend, or daydream.

It's a Saturday morning and you are working hard at cleaning out the garage. The kids find your old guitar in its dusty case and say, "Sing us a song, Dad, please?" Remember the good times you had playing that guitar? Go ahead. Put down your broom. Pick up the guitar and tune it. Play it! Be alive in the moment.

Taking time out for spontaneous fun gives your children the message that playfulness doesn't have to stop, ever. Play is infectious. And it's good for your heart!

So . . . whether you're grown-up or not, save some of your energy for everyday fun.

> Fly a kite
> Blow beautiful bubbles with colors in them
> Rock in a rocking chair
> Go spelunking
> Play hide-and-seek
> Go to the county fair
> Make up songs in the car
> Go for a hike — even just around the block — and look for
>   something new
> Tell jokes
> Play word games
> Bring out a surprise — homemade ice cream
> Add your own:

Any one of these may turn out to be a real heart-warmer.

Heart Time

Time spent with your child is a care package of memories-to-be. It includes basic interactions and ordinary spontaneous moments together. It is a package wrapped with acceptance and tied with love.

"When my dad went running, he'd let me ride my bike alongside."

"At Christmas time I helped Mom make candles to give."

"Some Saturday mornings Dad made us breakfast on an old-fashioned waffle iron."

"My aunt loved to play Scrabble with me."

"Grandpa took me fishing at the pier."

"We always knew there'd be family hugs and nose kisses."

Simple things are what children remember.

There is no minimum
daily requirement
for the amount of time
you spend with
your children.

Kids aren't the only ones to gather memories. Nothing can replace time spent together — shopping, talking, brunching, walking, working, or just watching the world go by. And adults, like children, very often remember the sentimental rather than the spectacular.

"Every year my son and I get season tickets. We cheer on the team — win or lose. Those are great times together."

"Whenever I meet my daughter downtown, we shop 'til our feet give out! We never buy much, but we laugh a lot!"

"Sometimes after the kids are in bed, my husband and I make a fire and popcorn just for us."

"My granddaughter stops by between college classes to visit. She likes to go through my photo albums and old clippings and dance programs from *my* college days."

"My son and I meet in December for a whole day to pore over cookbooks and try out new cookie recipes. We've come up with some real winners!"

"Family holidays are just as wonderful now that we're grown-up. Everyone has a special, traditional dish to bring."

"The whole family gets together over Labor Day to play music and sing — from Gramps and his harmonica to David and his electric bass! We're not great, but we have a terrific time."

The Heart Thermostat

Adults are climate-controllers. We know when situations are heating up and we know when we need to keep cool. When you're trying to create a comfort zone in family relationships, the best thermostat is your heart.

Here are some ideas:

1. Keep the channels open. People don't communicate if they expect to be criticized or lectured.

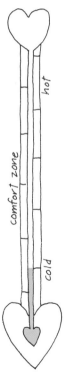

OPENERS	CLOSERS
Hmmmmmmmm . . .	I told you so!
That's really interesting . . .	That's terrible.
What do you think?	I won't allow it!
Can we talk?	NO!

2. Show your appreciation. Appreciation and consideration warm hearts—and keep the climate comfortable. There's nothing like a simple "thank you" to temper the small chills that can ice over any family's relationships now and then. Some samples:

"Thanks for starting supper—that was a big help."

"What a pal you are, Danny, for meeting me at the end of the walk with an umbrella! You rescued me from a real drenching!"

"Thanks for putting a shirt on before you came to the table."

"So, you're going to use the top shelf and your brother the bottom shelf. I'm proud of you both for figuring that out on your own."

"Boy, was I glad when I pulled in the drive and saw that all the bikes were put away."

"I noticed you did your chores without being asked." (Add a hug here.)

"I knew I married the right guy!"

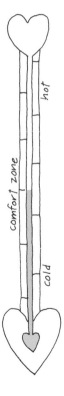

3. Monitor your reactions.

> Your husband (or wife) is late. Your sweet little girl has floured the kitchen floor with the sifter. Your teenager has missed curfew — again. How you respond to these situations will depend on many factors — how anxious you are (or how tired), what time you're expecting company, and whether or not the dog is unintentionally pregnant.

> It is okay to be angry.

> It is okay to remain calm.

> You decide where to set your thermostat. Observe your family's reactions too. You may choose to alter the temperature.

Remember that how you, as adults, relate to each other makes for a comfortable climate — just right for growing — or a nippy or steamy one. When anger heats up your home atmosphere, or resentment cools it down, children immediately feel the changes. Children reflect the environment you have created; they are more sensitive than thermometers.

You choose where to set your thermostat.

Wow! She loves me. I spilled the juice everywhere and she still loves me. She didn't say, "You're stupid. You're clumsy." She didn't say, "You know better than that." When it spilled, I felt sad. I was scared. She said, "Let's clean this up together." She said, "I'll bet that pitcher was heavy." She said, "Maybe next time I could help you." Wow! I love her.

Children need you
the most when they're
at their worst.

House of Hearts Specifications

Now's the time to check your construction. Is there a strong foundation of trust? Is the structure framed with realistic expectations and insulated with plenty of hugs and kisses? Remember that your building may need to expand to accommodate children's growth and stages — and adults' too. Remodel by tearing down walls of guilt and allowing added room for acceptance.

Basic construction needs also include:

a solid flooring of consideration
a warm heart for a heating system
custom pipes of praise
walls adorned with the colors and patterns of humor

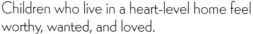

Children who live in a heart-level home feel worthy, wanted, and loved.

This is not just a heart-level home, but a way of life.

Heart-Savers

While building a House of Hearts for children to live in and develop their self-esteem, remember that adults, too, need to feel worthy, wanted, and loved.

Feelings and needs not considered build mountains of resentment. When you feel yourself being pulled under in the whirlpool of parenthood, try a heart-saver.

LAUGHTER

An evening out, a weekend out, a week out
A new novel
An outing with friends

LAUGHTER

Time alone
A class
A wonderful salad
    (make it just for you this time!)

LAUGHTER

The Heart of the Matter

When your child is twenty, he won't put Leggos down the toilet, suck his thumb, or drink bathwater — probably. She won't hide her hairbrush, poke her brother when nobody's looking, or maul the cat with overzealous love.

Someday your husband may not be cranky from pressures at work — or miss a kid's school conference because of "an important business meeting." Your wife won't always be frazzled and frayed around the edges from juggling job and motherhood.

This longer view is hard to envision in the midst of day-to-day living.

In the meantime, you can't afford to make life into more of a crisis than it already is. Try to keep it all in perspective.

People need each
other the most when they're
at their worst.

What compromises can you live with? *You* decide what is most important to *you*.

Do you want to be chairperson of the PTA? Or learn to skydive?

What is your idea of perfection? Must you have a superneat house? Or can you shut the door on a messy bedroom and think maybe someday the house will be clean? (Maybe, when the children leave home, you'll discover *you're* the messy one.)

Should you accept the promotion, change careers, or go back to college?

Are you alarmed or annoyed by your children's explorative and inquisitive behavior? Or do you ask yourself, What — or whom — is it hurting? Is all this investigating and questioning harmful to themselves or others? Is it destructive? If not, then let them explore. Children are natural explorers.

Supermoms and superdads
exist only on bumperstickers.

Choosing to cope
is better than the alternative.

He likes me just the way I am!

When I quit guitar lessons, he said, "Everyone's not into music."

When I didn't get a B in algebra, he said, "Math was hard for me too."

When I didn't make the soccer team, he said, "Let's go shoot some baskets."

When I said I wanted to draw cartoons instead of studying to be a doctor, he said, "Fine! When you really like what you do, you'll do it well."

He likes me just the way I am; it feels good to be me.

I like me just the way I am.

Children don't always turn out the way adults would like to design them. A loving heart accepts children as they *are*.

My wife's happy. She tells me that there is no place else she'd rather be. She likes my friends, even Ralph. And she never mentions that I'm going bald. She brags about me to her mother; she even brags about me to *my* mother. When I decided to change careers at forty, she said, "Honey, I just want you to be happy."

Heart-Testers and Heart-Warmers

Living with children includes the difficult and the joyous.

Eating the broken cookie, the collapsing popsicle, the burned toast — and taking the plate away because the gravy touched the applesauce.

Putting shoes on the same feet you've already put them on four times today.

Bursting with pride because he finally graduated.

Cutting her sandwich in half when she wanted it whole, and serving it whole when she wanted it cut in half.

Loving a child so much that you get misty with tears — and other times just wanting to cry from pure frustration.

Driving him to soccer practice . . . and driving him to soccer practice . . . and driving him to soccer practice . . . .

Remaking the costume because He-man doesn't wear a cape. Or adding wings to tennies because Wonder-girl doesn't wear ordinary Reeboks.

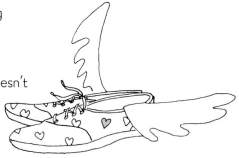

Living with adults includes the worrisome and the wonderful.

Thinking about someone else's schedule, preferences, interests — and *then* thinking about your own.

Getting an affectionate hug when you need it, or when you don't need it.

Taking the checkbook to him because he forgot it, again.

Having Thanksgiving dinner at your house . . . and having Thanksgiving dinner at your house . . . and having Thanksgiving dinner at your house.

Taking the car and discovering there's no gas in it.

Listening to her conference speech, over and over — and realizing just how good it really is.

Guilt-Erasers = Heart-Strengtheners

A good swipe of a guilt-eraser at the end of the day may help eradicate bad feelings.

It's been one of those days! Most of your verbal communication with the kids has been high-decibel and high-pitched. So it's an early supper and bath. And you can't wait for bedtime. The evening ends with a final yell from you—and a slammed door.

Then comes the guilt. You feel sorry and guilty for your behavior, and the children feel sorry and guilty for theirs. Now is the time to let go of your guilt and to help them let go of theirs.

When a power struggle puts you in a parental bind and your children in a state of resistance, how can you communicate heart-to-heart?

GUILT-ERASERS

Say, "I'm sorry," and explain YOUR point of view.

Hugs

Laughter

Prayers

Snuggles

Say, "I love you," and listen to THEIR point of view.

Use these same guilt-erasers with the adults in your life. They work with all ages.

Guilt is a heart-attacker.

When you make children feel guilty
you turn them into actors.
They portray themselves
in a role you have written.
Let them follow their own scripts.

When you make children
feel guilty they compromise
their integrity
for your love.

Language of the Heart

Never underestimate the power of politeness.

Just by speaking courteously, you may be able to bring out the very best in the people you live with. Give them a chance to talk. Listen patiently. And soften your voice. A soft voice can tame adult anger and smooth over teenage traumas.

As for little children — they love whispers. Stooping down to their level and looking directly into their eyes can make the difference between heartaches and heartsongs.

HEARTACHES	HEARTSONGS
You didn't stay inside the lines.	That's special. I can see that you worked hard.
Look how dirty you are!	Looks like you had fun today.
What's that supposed to be?	I like black.
NO!	Let's talk about that before we decide.
Get over here right now!	I need you with me.
I TOLD YOU SO.	That was harder than you thought.

For older children:

HEARTACHES	HEARTSONGS

Shut your door when you
play that awful music!

Is that a new tape
you're playing? Who is it?

You're wearing that same
old sweater – *again*?

You look really handsome today.

If you think I'm going to let you
do *that,* think again! I know
what goes on! I was your age
once.

It will probably be okay.
Get all the details.
And then we'll
decide.

What have you *done* to your hair?

Looks like you feel a little
crazy today.

You listen to me!

I need to tell you how I feel.

I TOLD YOU SO.

The same thing happened
to me once.

For grown-ups:

HEARTACHES	HEARTSONGS
I hate that wallpaper sample. I can't understand why you like it.	Let's look at some more.
You never seem to have any time for me! You're always in that workshop of yours!	Let's plan on doing something together this weekend — something we both like.
How come you're so late?	Did you have a hard day?
I TOLD YOU SO.	I'm really sorry it didn't work out.

Heart-to-Heart Talk

What's the magic word?

Say excuse me.

What do you say?

As parents we often fall into the trap of criticizing our children's social skills. Most of the time young children simply won't know what to say or do in social situations. They need help — not just prompting. Try having a heart-to-heart talk before such occasions arise.

It will make Grandma feel good if you tell her you love her.

It's polite to say please and thank you.

When we meet someone, we look up and say hello.

If you hurt somebody's feelings, the person will feel better if you say you're sorry.

If a child's proper response doesn't materialize at the right moment, a parent can respond instead:

> We love you, Grandma.
>
> Thank you for both of us.
>
> Hello. We're glad to meet you.
>
> I'm sorry that happened.

Your children will be likely to follow your example – eventually.

Heart Rate

Everyone in a family moves at a different pace. Of course, fast-movers are inclined to get impatient with deliberate, methodical ones. When a young person seems to be operating on tortoise time, it's easy for a parent to overload the child with directives. A heart response instead of a hasty response will ease anxieties when family tempos need to be in sync.

HASTY RESPONSE	HEART RESPONSE
I've got to rush – 'bye.	I'm really going to miss you today, but I know you'll be having fun here.
If you ask me one more time, we're not going!	I know you're excited, but we have to wait. I'll let you know when it's almost time.
Hurry…you'll be late for school. Find your shoes and socks. Get your books. Don't forget your gym clothes. Get out to the car!	Bus leaves in eight minutes.
Turn off the TV – NOW!	When this program is over, you'll need to turn off the TV and get ready to go.

Humor can speed children along when their pace doesn't match yours.

*I need you out of the tub now. Get ready for the
drying machine — here it comes!*

Heart-Provers

For older children and adults in your family, sometimes allowing consequences to happen is the kindest way to bring your slowpokes up to tempo. All your shouting and prodding can never be as effective as a missed schoolbus, forgotten gym clothes (and a demerit in P.E.), or being late for work and having to deal with the boss.

Consequences work wonders. Consequences are heart-provers; letting them happen proves you care.

Learning by Heart

I want to walk by myself.

I want to hold the umbrella.

No! Let me do it.

A child develops autonomy by being allowed to be independent and accomplish tasks without interference or help. Parents often hear children say, "No, I want to do it myself!" and interpret this statement as an act of defiance. For children, this is a normal and important step toward the development of themselves as separate, fully functioning human beings.

When we allow children to do for themselves and then laud their efforts, they develop competence and a readiness to tackle tasks ahead.

Sometimes a child's
saying no means little more
than the child's desire
to find out
how it feels
to say no.

I dressed myself. I put on one red sock and one blue sock because red and blue are pretty. My mom says that's okay.

I put on my pants and put the pocket in the front so the lace would show. My mom says a pocket should be where you can see it.

When I put on my sweater, there was an extra button left over at the bottom. But Mom says it will be even when I'm older.

I picked out the purple headband because my grandma sent it to me in the mail. Mom says you can wear any color headband you want.

I dressed myself. She said I looked like a rainbow . . . and Mom says rainbows are beautiful.

I passed my driver's test!

Heart-Building Exercises

1. Your child comes home from school and tells you that a boy hit him.

    a. You call the school immediately and report that someone is picking on your child.

    b. You lecture him not to play with that bad boy again.

    c. You listen. Find out who was hit first . . . why . . . and how hard.

2. Your child is absorbed in making mudpies outside. You would like her to come in to see a nature special on TV because she will learn something important.

    a. You tell her to get in the house and clean up because you have something worthwhile for her to do.

    b. You decide that she's as close to nature right now as she can get.

3. Your three children have just taken all of the cushions off the couch and are tussling on them.

    a. You lose your cool. It's a brand-new couch, and you already set up the no-dismantling rule. All three get in trouble.

    b. You redirect them to another activity, giving them the choice of a quiet indoor activity or going outside.

    c. You provide some old cushions and let them pounce on them in a specified place where they can't get hurt or hurt anything else.

4. You take the kids on vacation and on the way home you're happy they remember:

    a. The Grand Canyon.

    b. The Smithsonian Institution.

    c. The comic books they read in the car.

    d. Whatever good memory they may have.

5. Your son announces that he wishes his Aunt Sally was really his mother instead of you.

    a. You are crushed. He must love her more than he loves you.

    b. You say to him, "What a horrible, awful thing to say to your mother!"

    c. You listen patiently as he explains that it's because she lives in an apartment with STAIRS.

6. Your daughter comes from preschool with a painting. You say:

    a. "What is it?"

    b. "You only painted one corner of the paper."

    c. "Didn't they have any other color besides blue?"

    d. "Blue is my favorite color."

7. Your teenage son comes home from school and tells you about a friend who takes drugs.

   a. You panic and launch into your anti-drug lecture—again.

   b. You say, "You're not allowed to associate with that kid ever again!" And you mean it.

   c. You're surprised. You ask your son, "What do you think about that?" Then you continue to listen . . . and listen.

8. You think you are never going to make it through your daughter's teen years and her defiant attitude.

   a. You scrutinize her friends and monitor her every move.

   b. You ignore her and hope for the best.

   c. No matter how difficult it seems, EVERY DAY you hug her and say, "I love you."

Living from the Heart

We're all human and we all need love. We need to find ways to meet each other at heart level. Here are some heart-warming words from families we know:

> A young child says to her mother, "You make me beautiful, Mom." Her mother asks, "Because I fix your hair with ribbons?" "No," says the child. "Because you teach me about love."

> A twelve-year-old writes, "Dear Dad, thanks for everything. I love you. It's the best I can give."

> A teenager admits, "I thought I'd be embarrassed, Mom, because you were around, but my friends thought you were really neat."

Little children live from the heart. So do older children and grown-ups — although it's sometimes harder to tell.

When we discover this, and reach each other from the heart, we're all happier.

A House of Hearts
makes everyone
who lives there
feel good.

About the Authors

Doris Jasinek has spent twenty years as a teacher, administrator, camp director, consultant, and lecturer. For fourteen years she has been director of Bethlehem Community Preschool in Encinitas, California. Her Let's Explore parenting class was the inspiration for this book.

She studied at University of California in San Diego, San Diego State University, and University of London, where she learned about British infant schools. She has two grown children and three grandchildren.

Pamela Bell Ryan is a graduate of Bakersfield Junior College and San Diego State University, where she is now working toward a master's degree in education. She has been involved in early childhood education as a bilingual teacher, assistant director, and volunteer coordinator for Red Cross refugee playschools. She is editor of the Encinitas library's newsletter, *The Friend Ship*, written by and for elementary school children. She and Doris serve on a committee for the Bethelehem Lutheran Church Expansion Project, which will encompass a community care center for children and seniors.

She and her husband, Jim, live in Leucadia, California. Their lively household also includes daughters aged ten and six, and twin four-and-a-half-year-old boys.